Yellowstone National Park

Attractions & Sights to See

Billy Grinslott & Kinsey Marie Books

ISBN - 9781960612984

Touring the Grand Loop at Yellowstone can be exciting. You may get the opportunity to take photos of animals out your car window. Besides riding in your own car, there are bus tours you can take. Either way it will be fun to bc able to take pictures of animals and Bison close up.

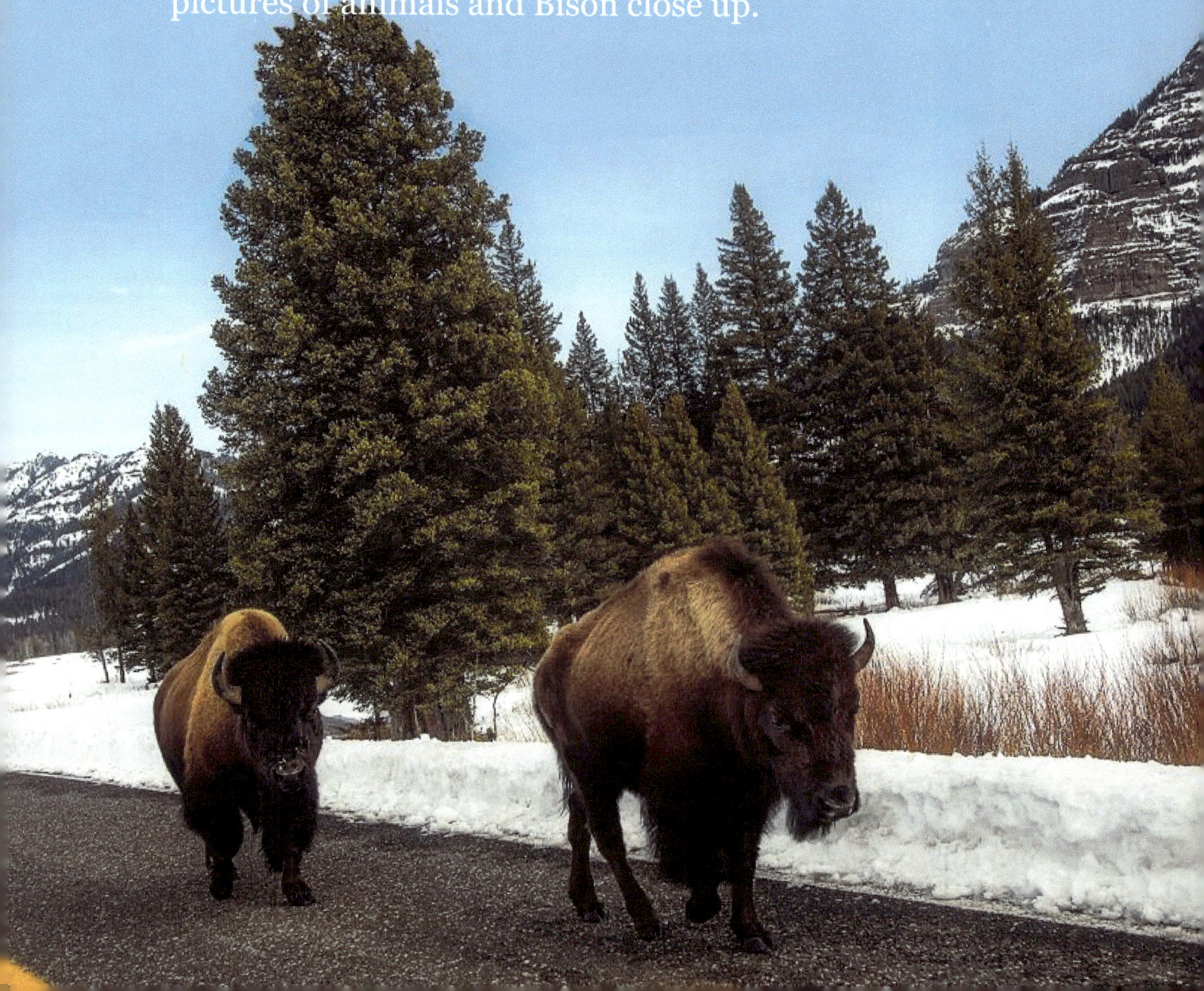

Hayden Valley. This valley, centrally located in Yellowstone National Park, is the first place to go to see wildlife in Yellowstone. As you drive along this beautiful, broad valley you are likely to see herds of bison, scattered elk, and the occasional grizzly bear. You are also likely to see waterfowl, including ducks, Canada geese and pelicans, swimming in or lounging near the Yellowstone River.

The Black Sand Basin is named for the black sand in the area, composed of obsidian, a volcanic glass. Which is formed when lava cools too quickly. It is located in the Upper Geyser Basin. The Upper Geyser Basin has the largest concentration of geysers in the world. The Upper Geyser Basin consists of several different sections, including Old Faithful, Geyser Hill, Castle Geyser, Morning Glory Pool, Black Sand Basin, and Biscuit Basin. This is a picture of Morning Glory Pool.

Midway Geyser Basin contains a small collection of mammoth-sized springs. Midway is part of the Lower Geyser Basin. This is a picture of the Grand prismatic spring. Hot water travels 121 feet from a crack in the earth to reach the surface of the spring. The grand prismatic is the third largest spring in the world.

Terrace Springs are located along the Terrace Springs Trail. Terrace Spring is a small, pretty thermal area north of Madison. There is a short boardwalk that provides a tour of the hot springs area.

Sapphire Pool. This is one of the more memorable pools in the park. It has bright blue clear water. Sapphire Pool use to be an active geyser prior to the 1959 earthquake. After the earthquake, the gorgeous pool filled with water and began to have larger eruptions. It wasn't until 1971 that the pool stopped having eruptions.

Mammoth Hot Springs is a large complex of hot springs and terraces on travertine hill. These features are quite different from thermal areas elsewhere in the park. Travertine formations grow much more rapidly due to the softer nature of limestone. As hot water rises through limestone, large quantities of rock are dissolved by the hot water, and a white chalky mineral is deposited on the surface.

Tower-Roosevelt to Lamar Valley. Lamar Valley is an excellent place to view wildlife, with it being one of the major summer grounds for many animals. Visitors have the chance to spot herds of bison, elk, antelope, bighorn sheep, mule deer, wolf packs, and various bird species. Lamar Valley is known for it's abundant wildlife especially the Bison. Best time to visit is early in the morning.

Obsidian cliff. Obsidian is found in volcanic areas where magma is rich in silica or sand and the lava has cooled to fast without forming crystals, creating a black glass look. Obsidian cliff is made out of Obsidian and that's how it got it's name. Obsidian Cliff has an exposed vertical thickness of about 98 feet. You can find it along Grand Loop Road, which runs through the park.

Sheepeater Cliff. The basalt of Sheepeater Cliff are known as columnar basalt due to the hexagonal fracture lines that formed in the basalt when it cooled. Sheepeater Cliff is made up of columnar basalt deposited by lava flows roughly 500,000 years ago. The cliff and associated picnic area are named after the Tukudika, or Sheep Eaters, a band of Eastern Shoshone Indians. It's a 1 mile roundtrip easy hike.

Mount Washburn is one of the most popular day hikes in the park and with good reason. The trail climbs 1,400 feet of modcrate switchbacks with diverse plant life and open views along the way. The 10,243-foot summit offers an endless panorama views from the Tetons to the Grand Canyon of the Yellowstone and beyond. 6.8-mile out-and-back trail considered a moderately challenging route.

Yellowstone River. At 692 miles, the Yellowstone is the longest free-flowing river in the Lower 48 states. Its headwaters in the southern Absaroka Mountains are located as far from a road as you can get in the Continental U.S. The Gallatin, Madison, Snake, Shoshone, Clarks Fork, and Fall River are all major rivers originating in Yellowstone National Park.

Tower falls is in the northeastern part of Yellowstone near Tower Junction. the fall plunges an amazing 132 feet. Enjoy this 1-mile out-and-back trail near Gardiner, Montana. considered a moderately challenging route. A half-mile steep, switchback hike downward takes you to the bottom of the waterfall. Tower Fall was named in for the stunning, rocky side walls that frame the falls.

Upper and Lower Falls. The Lower Falls can be seen from Artist Point and Uncle Tom's Trail and the Upper Falls can be seen from the Upper Fall Viewing Area. You will have fun hiking to both these spots.

If you're driving between Norris Geyser Basin and Madison Junction, take a quick stop to see Gibbon Falls. Gibbon Falls drops 84 feet over the remnants of the caldera rim. The caldera rim was created by a volcanic eruption that happened about 600 thousand years ago. Park in the lot near the top of the falls but be ready to wait your turn as the lot is often crowded. There is also a half mile trail you can take to get more views.

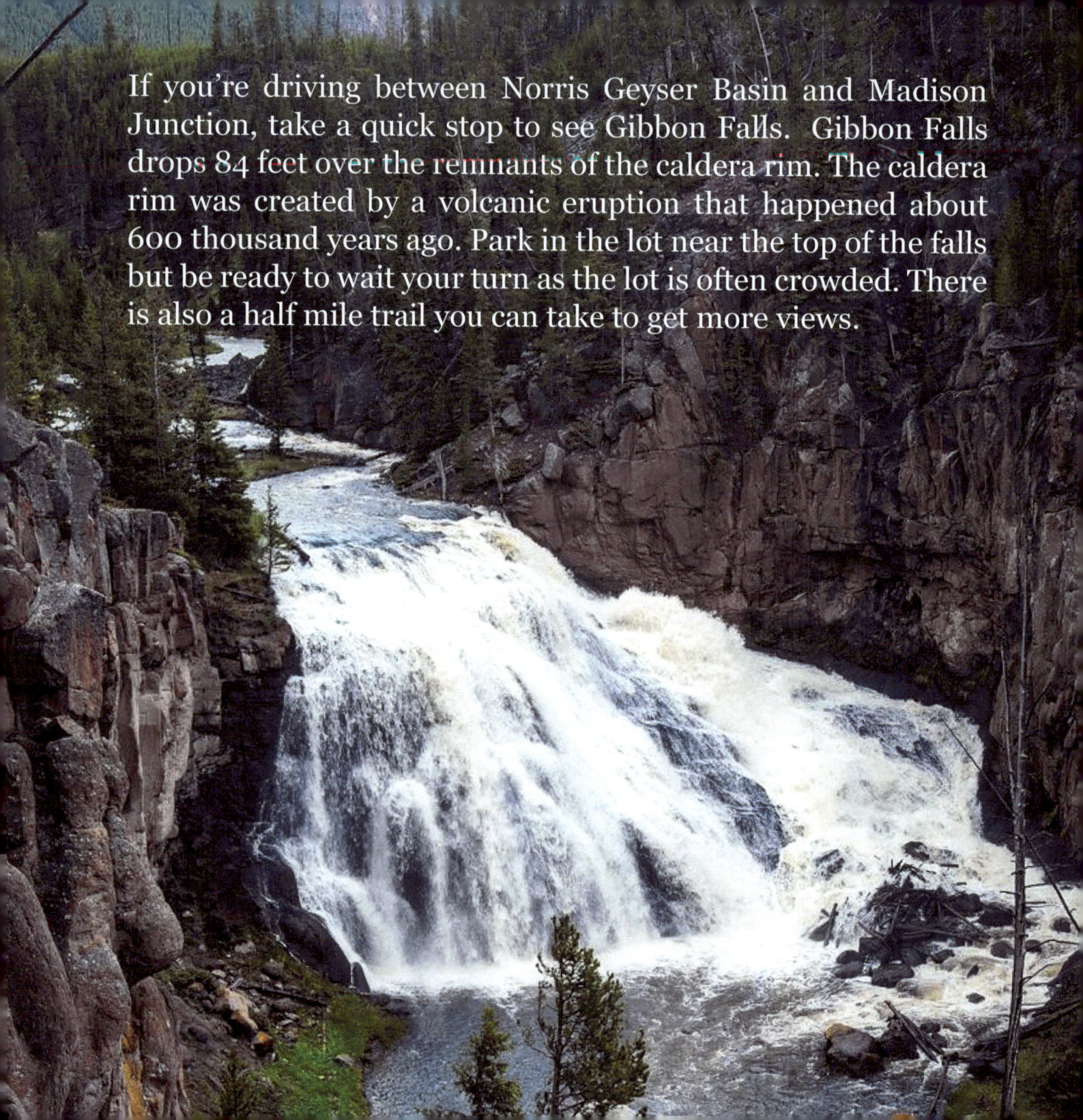

The Lamar River is located entirely within Yellowstone National Park. The Lamar River runs 45 miles from its source to the Yellowstone River. There are many access areas. You can enjoy water sports, fishing and camping, or take a guided hike.

The Golden Gate Canyon runs between Mammoth Hot Springs and the Yellowstone Plateau. Right off the Grand Loop Road in between Norris and Mammoth it offers inspiring views of the canyon and the valley, there is smallish falls on one side and massive golden rock wall on the other side. Awesome views along this road.

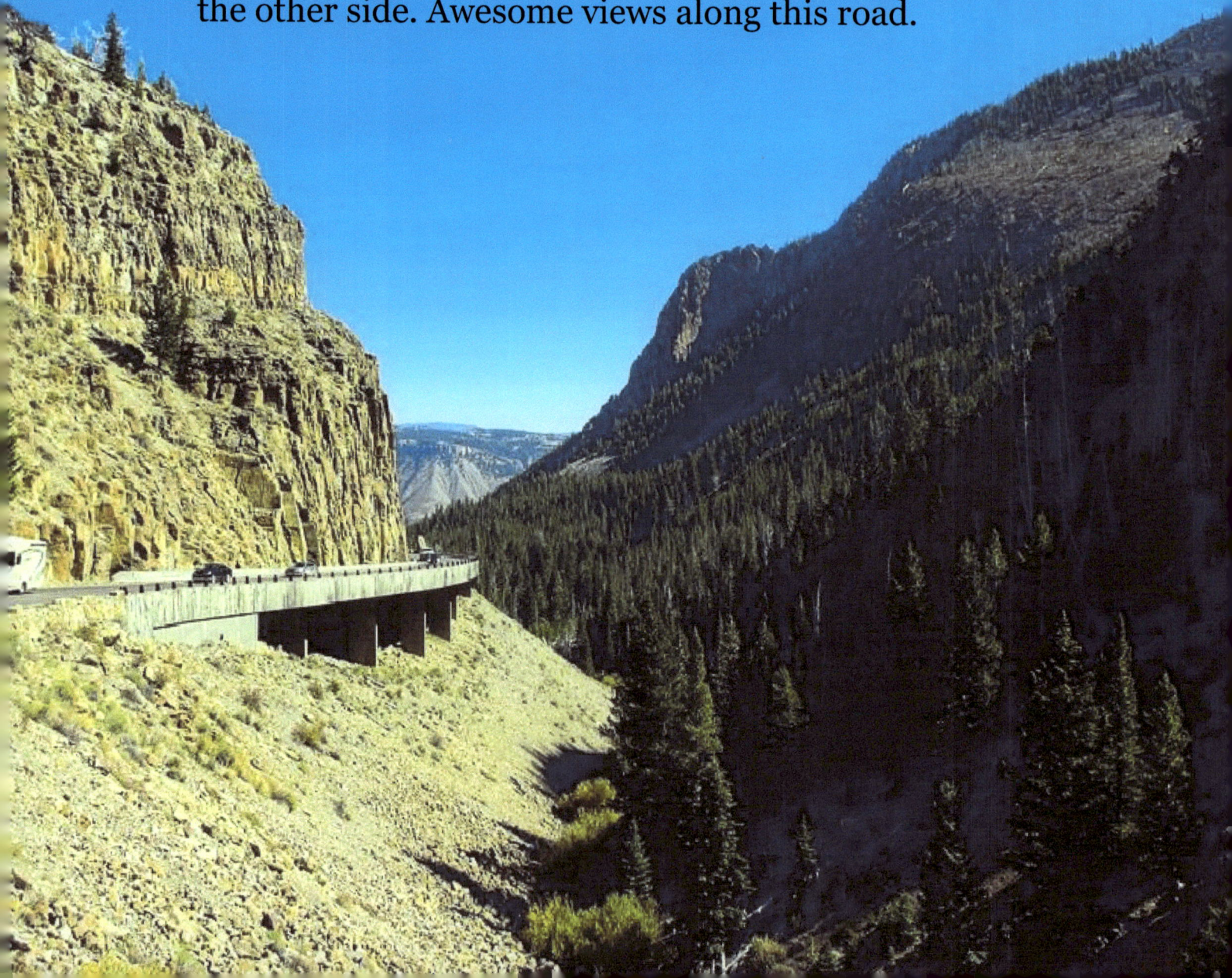

Grand Canyon of Yellowstone Park. Not to be confused with the real Grand Canyon in Arizona, this is still a great site to see. The Lower Falls of the Yellowstone River cascades down over 300 feet into the steep ravine. It's roughly 20 miles long, measured from the Upper Falls to the Tower Fall area. It's a great spot to see the twists of the Yellowstone River below and to appreciate the contrasting colors of the canyon.

Yellowstone Lake is the largest high elevation lake in North America. The lake covers 136 square miles with 110 miles of shoreline. Due to the thermal activity in the park, most rivers and lakes in Yellowstone are closed to swimmers. However, if you're up for an adventure, the park has opened up a few alluring areas to the public. The structure under the water is different than most lakes, it's made up of volcanic crustaceans caused by volcanic activity.

Grizzly and wolf discovery center in West Yellowstone is a great way to take a tour and see the animals. It takes Two to three hours but gives you the best chance to see animals feeding, plus the exhibition center is interesting.

Mud Volcano is a major geyser area on the east half of Yellowstone National Park, containing one of our favorite thermal features. Dragon's Mouth Spring is a spot where boiling water has gradually eroded away the hillside, creating a cavern that resounds constantly with flowing waters, almost like there really is a dragon lurking in there.

The Boiling River is a stream of hot water pouring over a rock ledge into the Gardner River. Users have piled rocks to create a soaking area where the 140-degree water mixes with the cold river. It is the perfect Yellowstone Park hot springs swimming experience.

West Thumb Geyser Basin, including Potts Basin is the largest geyser basin on the shores of Yellowstone Lake. West Thumb has less geyser activity than other basins. But for its size, it has a lot of hot springs, majestic pools, mud pots, fumaroles and lake shore geysers. Fishing Cone has been the most popular feature in West Thumb Geyser Basin. This area has a 1 mile loop you can walk and see the views.

Biscuit geyser Basin is located two miles northwest of Old Faithful Village on the western side of the Grand Loop Road. The basin is within the Yellowstone Caldera area and has numerous hot pools and geysers. One of the most famous features is a blue-colored hot spring named Sapphire Pool. It has a 1 mile loop you can walk to see the sights.

Black Pool Started out as a dark color and that's how it got its name. But it has changed in color over the years due to its temperature getting warmer. Black Pool remains hot, and is now one of Yellowstone's most beautiful and intensely blue pools. It is located in the West Thumb Geyser Basin loop.

The Fountain Paint Pot is one of many mud pots found in the park. In early summer the mud pots are thin and watery from abundant rain and snow. By late summer they are thicker. The mud is composed of clay minerals and fine particles of sand. The Fountain Paint Pot parking area is next to the Firehole Lake Road. It has a half mile trail to explore the area.

The Grand Prismatic Spring is in the Midway Geyser Basin in Yellowstone Park. It is the largest hot spring in the United States. The vibrant colors are the result of the microbial life that live along the edges of the hot spring. The colors can change depending upon the presence of different types of microbes and the temperature of the water. The trail to the overlook is where this picture is from, is 1.5 miles. Or you can walk from the parking lot to the spring.

Caldera Volcano. Yellowstone Park sits over a super volcano that is capable of an eruption of a magnitude 8. It has had three massive eruptions, all of which created calderas. A caldera is a large volcanic crater, formed by a major eruption leading to the collapse of the mouth of the volcano. If the volcano erupts again, it will have devastating effects causing the air to fill up with ash and the effect will be a huge climate change Worldwide.

Lower Geyser Basin contains hundreds of hot pools and geysers. It is the largest geyser basin in the park. It is home to approximately 100 geothermal features. Combined, these features cover five square miles and include all four types of features, including fumaroles, hot springs, geysers, and mud pots.

Riverside Geyser. Situated on the bank of the Firehole River, Riverside Geyser is one of the most picturesque geysers in the park. The geyser shoots steam and water to heights of 75 feet in an arch over the river, sometimes causing rainbows. Riverside Geyser is about a mile hike from Old Faithful.

When active, the Beehive Geyser typically erupts once or twice a day and lasts about 4 to 5 minutes. The narrow cone acts like a jetting nozzle, projecting a powerful water stream to a height of 150-200 feet. You can hike the Upper Geyser Basin loop from old faithful to visit this geyser.

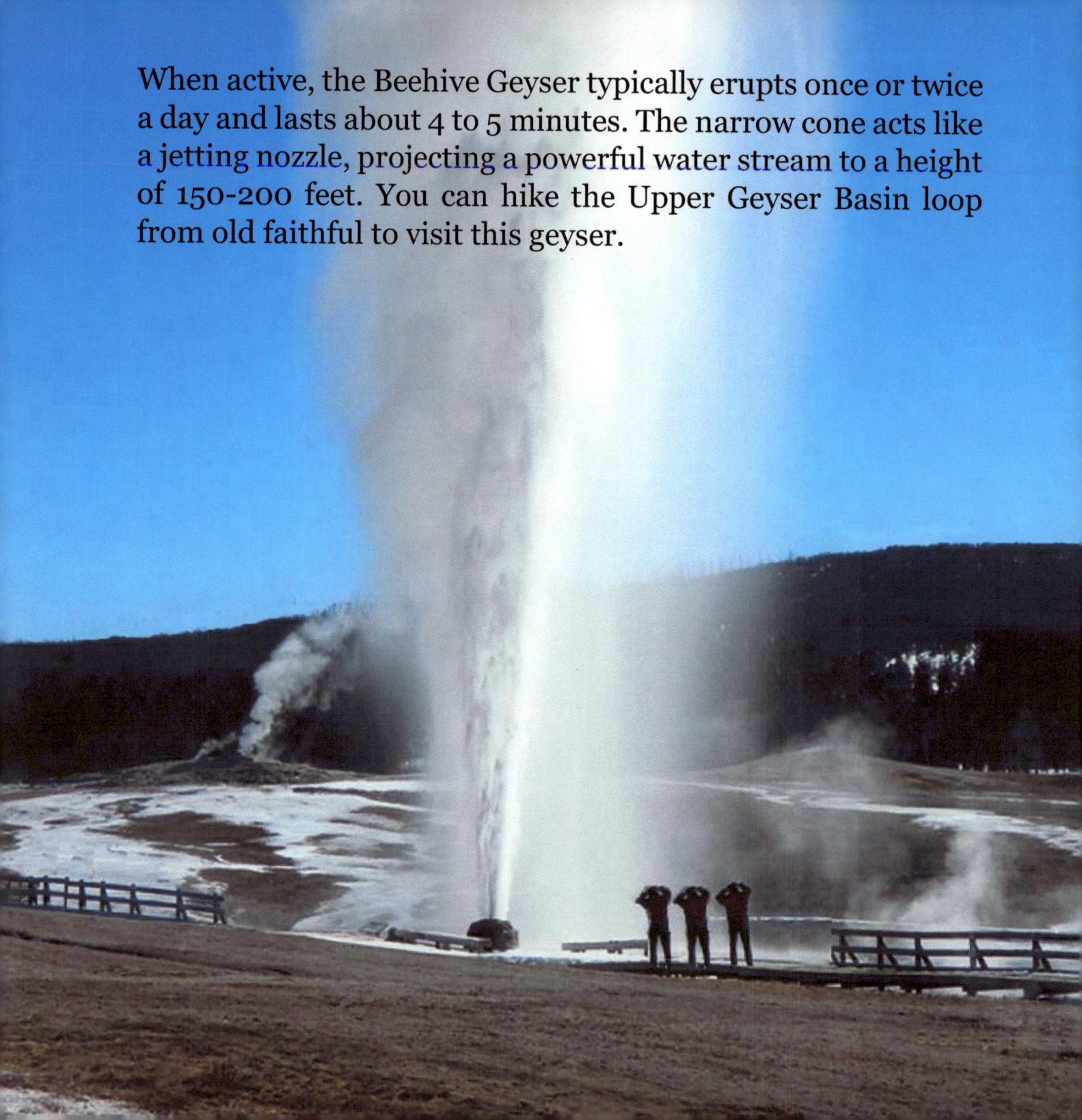

Lone Star Geyser erupts up to 45 feet. It has a 12-foot cone and erupts about every three hours and lasts about 30 minutes. The hike to the Lone Star Geyser is flat, making it easy to walk or ride a bike. The hike or bike to Lone Star is along an old road and is an easy, about a 5-mile round trip.

Great Fountain Geyser eruptions average 100 feet high, with some super bursts of 200 feet or more. Eruptions last 45-60 minutes in a series of bursts. Great Fountain Geyser takes 10-14 hours to rebuild to an eruption. The pool slowly fills and then begins to overflow about an hour before the eruption. Great Fountain Geyser experiences periods of irregularity. But, for the most part, it is dependable. It is in the Lower Geyser Basin of Yellowstone Park.

Castle Geyser has the largest cone and is one of the oldest geysers in the park. Its eruption pattern has changed considerably throughout history. Castle erupts about every 10 to 12 hours. The eruption can reach 90 feet and lasts about 20 minutes. It's about a 10 min walk from Old Faithful.

Grand Geyser erupts with powerful bursts rather than a steady column of water like Old Faithful. The average eruption lasts 9-12 minutes and consists of multiple bursts, usually reaching 150 to 200 feet in height. It has sporadic timing and erupts every 7 to 15 hours. It is in the Upper Geyser Basin not far from Old Faithful.

Norris Geyser Basin is the oldest, and most dynamic of Yellowstone's thermal areas. Steamboat Geyser in Norris Geyser Basin is the world's tallest active geyser at 300 feet. In 2018 it erupted more times than in any other year. It now erupts about every 5 days. Norris Basin has its own parking lot and a 1.8-mile easy loop trail.

The most famous attraction in Yellowstone is the Old Faithful Geyser. Old Faithful geyser was named for its frequent and somewhat predictable eruptions, which number more than a million times. An eruption lasts 2 to 5 minutes and expels 3,700–8,400 gallons of boiling water and reaches a height of 106–184 feet. Old Faithful Geyser has an average temperature of 169 degrees. It erupts around 20 times a day. There is a parking lot for old faithful that fills up fast. Or there are other trails you can hike that have different lengths.

Visitor Centers & Museums. Old Faithful Visitor Center, Canyon Visitor Education Center, Fishing Bridge Museum & Visitor Center, Grant Village Visitor Center, Madison Information Station, Albright Visitor Center, Norris Area Museums, West Yellowstone Visitor Center.

Things to Do. There is several different Geyser Basins you can visit, Drive the Park Roads, Hike the Trails, take a Guided Tour, Watch Wildlife, Take Photographs, Attend Events, join a Junior Ranger Program, Enjoy a Picnic, Bike in the Park, Ride a Horse, Camp in the Backcountry, Go Fishing, Boat or Kayak on a Lake, Swim and Soak.

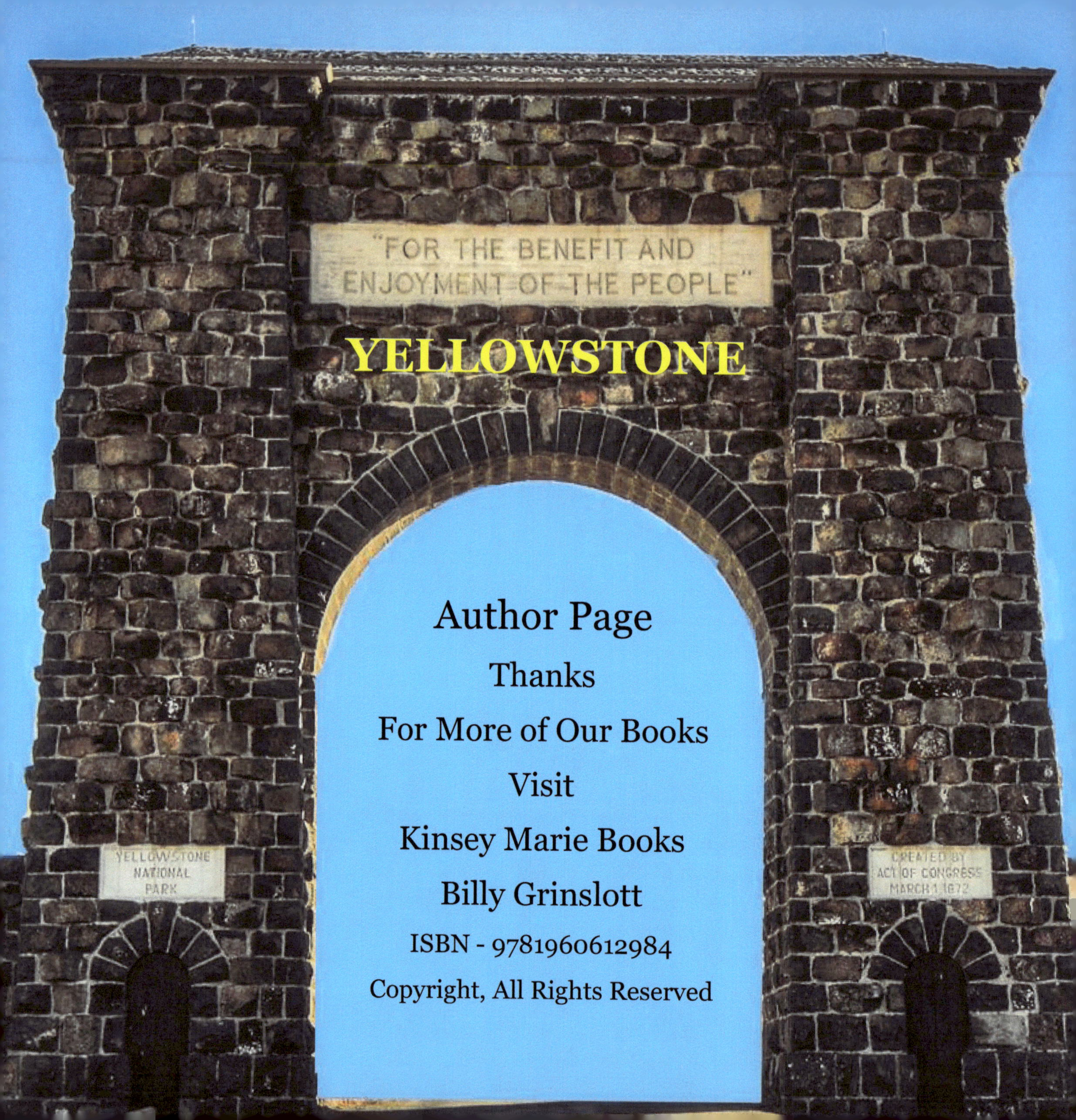
"FOR THE BENEFIT AND
ENJOYMENT OF THE PEOPLE"
YELLOWSTONE
NATIONAL
PARK
CREATED BY
ACT OF CONGRESS
MARCH 1 1872

YELLOWSTONE

Author Page

Thanks

For More of Our Books

Visit

Kinsey Marie Books

Billy Grinslott

ISBN - 9781960612984

www.ingramcontent.com/pod-product-compliance
Lightning Source LLC
Chambersburg PA
CBHW060852270326
41934CB00002B/111